All About The Record

The recorder is a very old instrument. The recorder was popular during the 16th and 17th centuries. Many famous composers of that time, including **Bach**, **Handel**, and **Telemann**, wrote music for the recorder. The recorder is made in different sizes. The smallest is a **garklein** recorder that is only six inches long! It is difficult to play because of the tiny holes, so the **descant** or **sopranino** recorder is used more often for the highest notes. There is also an **alto**, **tenor** and a **bass** recorder. These five recorders can play five part music, just like a choir can sing in four or five parts. A recorder choir is called a **consort**.

All the recorders have eight holes. The LEFT hand covers the thumb hole at the back of the recorder and the first three holes. The RIGHT hand covers the four holes at the bottom of the recorder. (Some recorders have divided holes at the bottom.)

Sound is made by blowing softly into the recorder mouthpiece. It is very easy to overblow the recorder and make a harsh ugly sound. Blowing softly and steadily makes the best sound. Each note should be started with the syllable 'doo' or 'too.' This is called **tonguing** the note. The air should be continuous, interrupted only briefly by the tongue when a new note is begun.

How to Care For the Recorder

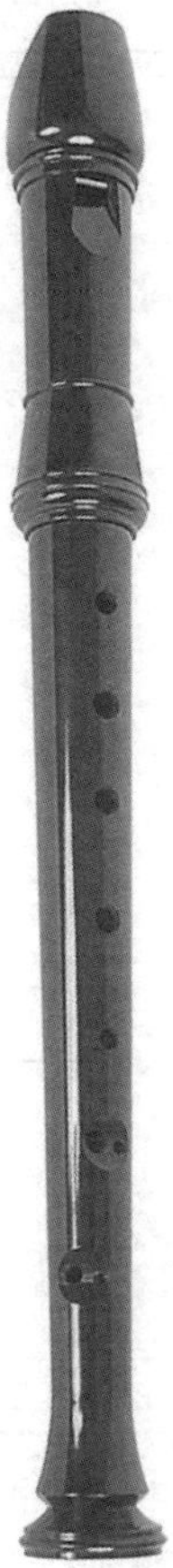

1. Recorders all look alike. Put your name on your recorder and on your case with a permanent marker. If you forget your recorder in the music room, your teacher will know it is yours.

2. Be careful not to bang the recorder against anything. Plastic can chip or crack.

3. Keep the mouthpiece clean. You can use a small brush or a pipe cleaner and water to wash out your mouthpiece.

4. Plastic recorders can be washed once in a while in warm, soapy water.

5. If your recorder is hard to put together, you can put a little Vaseline on the joints. If the joints are clean, they shouldn't need anything.

6. Keep your recorder in its case when you are not using it.

7. After playing, clean out the inside of your recorder with a narrow piece of cloth wound around the cleaning rod.

Supplies Needed to Care for the Recorder:

* A cleaning rod and a narrow piece of cloth
* A small mouthpiece brush or a pipe cleaner

How Notes are Named

Music is written on a staff. The staff has five lines. Notes can be written on each of the lines, or in the spaces between the lines.

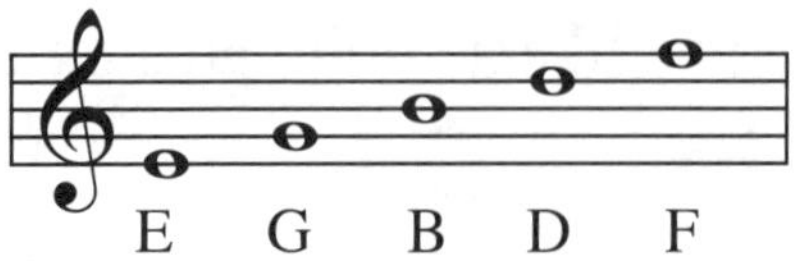

E G B D F

Notes on Lines

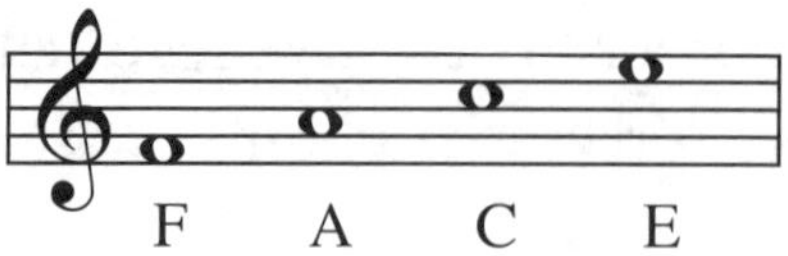

F A C E

Notes in Spaces

There is a clef at the beginning of every staff. The clef used for the recorder is the treble clef. The treble clef circles the note G, and is sometimes called the G clef. The first seven letters of the alphabet, A-G, are used to name notes. Notes are named in order - A B C D E F G. After G is named, the letters are used again beginning with A.

C D E F G A B C

Practice Naming Notes: Write the letter name of each note on the line below it. The first two notes are done for you.

E F ___ ___ ___ ___ ___ ___ ___ ___ ___ ___

F ___ ___ ___ ___ ___ ___ ___ ___ ___ ___ ___

Counting Music

The table below shows most of the notes you will be using in this recorder method. It tells the name of the note, a rhythm name that you can call it, and how many beats the note will get in 4/4 time.

Quarter note	♩	(ta)	1 beat
Pair of eighth notes	♫	(ti-ti)	together = 1 beat
Half note	𝅗𝅥	(too-oo)	2 beats
Dotted half note	𝅗𝅥.	(three-ee-ee)	3 beats
Whole note	𝅝	(fo-o-o-our)	4 beats

A rest is a silent beat. The table below shows most of the rests you will be using in this recorder method. It tells the name of the rest, a rhythm name that you can call it, and how many beats the rest will get in 4/4 time.

Quarter rest	𝄽	(sh)	1 beat
Half rest	𝄼	(re-est)	2 beats
Whole rest	𝄻	(re-e-e-est)	4 beats

To Do: Tell how many beats each note or rest is held for:

1. ♩	___ beat(s)		5. 𝄼	___ beat(s)
2. 𝄽	___ beat(s)		6. 𝅗𝅥.	___ beat(s)
3. 𝅝	___ beat(s)		7. ♫	___ beat(s)
4. 𝅗𝅥	___ beat(s)		8. 𝄻	___ beat(s)

Music is divided into short sections called **measures** or **bars**. The measures are marked off by **bar lines**. There is a **double bar line** at the end of each piece of music.

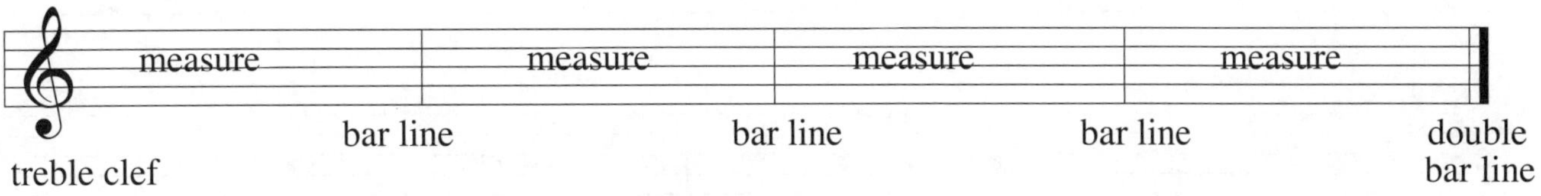

Let's Begin:

Whisper this pattern: doo doo doo doo doo....doo..... doo doo doo doo doo.......
When you say doo, your tongue lets the air out. This is called tonguing. You should blow into your recorder the same way, connecting the notes.

Cover the hole at the back of the recorder with your left thumb, and the top hole of the recorder with your left pointer finger and play this pattern on the note B.

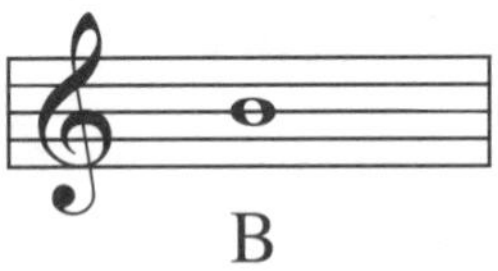
B

Always blow gently.....whisper warm air into the recorder.

1. Just B

2 bar intro

Denise Gagné

Cover the hole at the back of the recorder with your left thumb, and the top two holes of the recorder with your pointer and middle fingers and play this pattern on the note A:

Remember to blow gently and to begin each note with doo.

A

2. Just A

2 bar intro

Denise Gagné

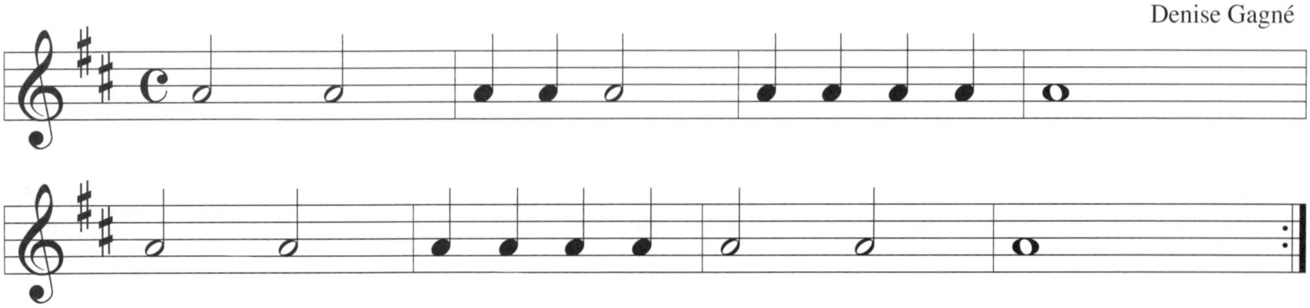

3. A and B Blues

2 bar intro

Denise Gagné

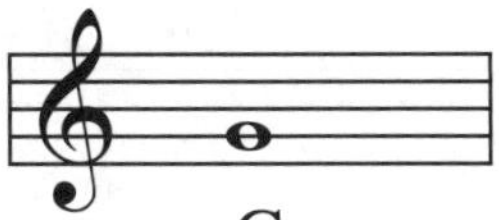

G

4. Just G

2 bar intro

Denise Gagné

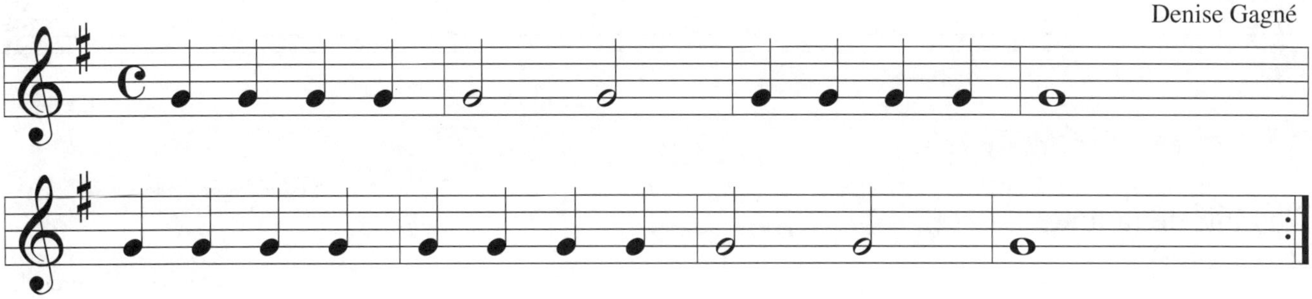

Name Your Notes:

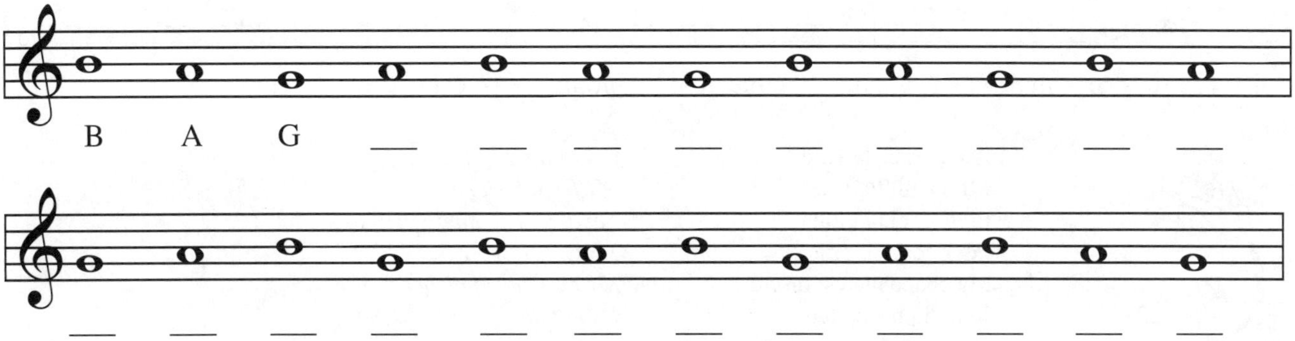

5. G and A Blues
2 bar intro

Denise Gagné

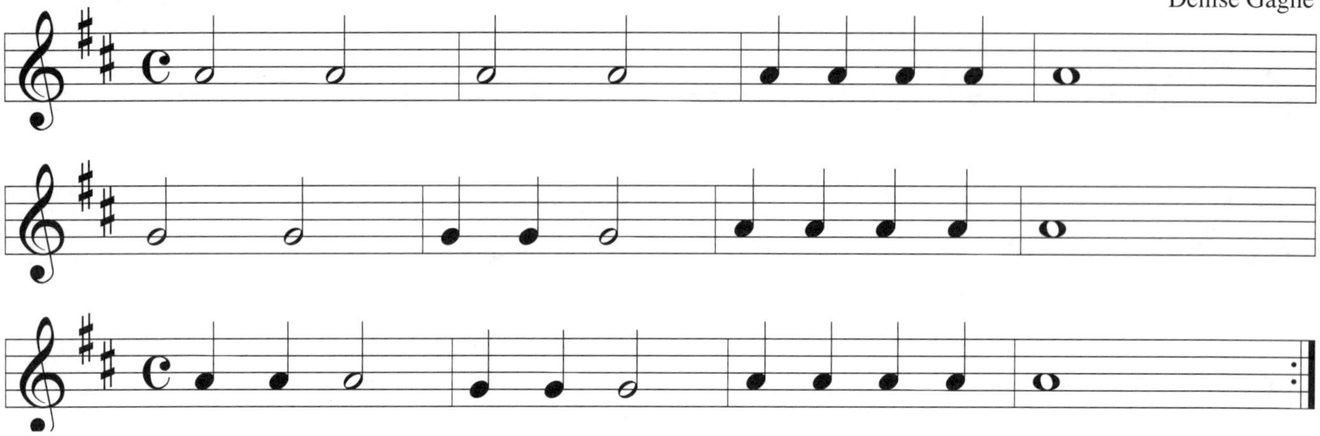

6. Side Step
2 bar intro

Denise Gagné

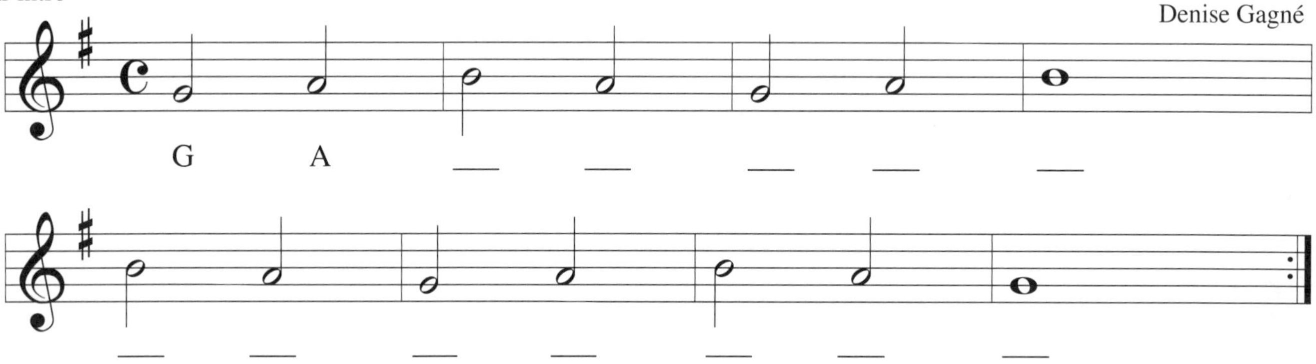

7. Au clair de la lune
2 bar intro (repeats)

French

Au clair de la lune	*In the light of the moon*
Mon ami Pierrot,	*My friend Pierrot,*
Prête-moi ta plume	*Lend your feather (pen) to me*
Pour écrire un mot.	*To write a word.*
Ma chandelle est morte,	*My candle is finished*
Je n'ai plus de feu.	*I don't have any fire. (light)*
Ouvre-moi ta porte,	*Open your door to me,*
Pour l'amour de Dieu!	*For the love of God!*

8. Hot Cross Buns Theme and Variations

2 bar intro

Theme:

Traditional

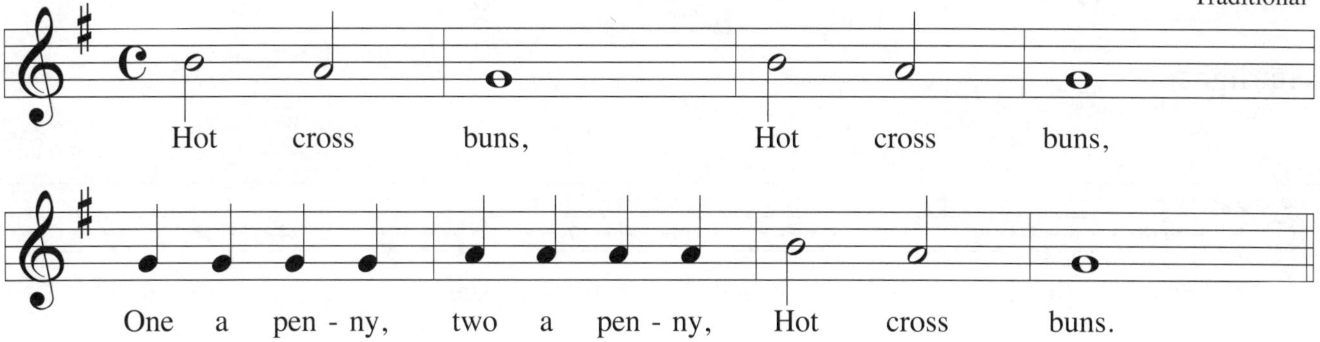

Variation 1:

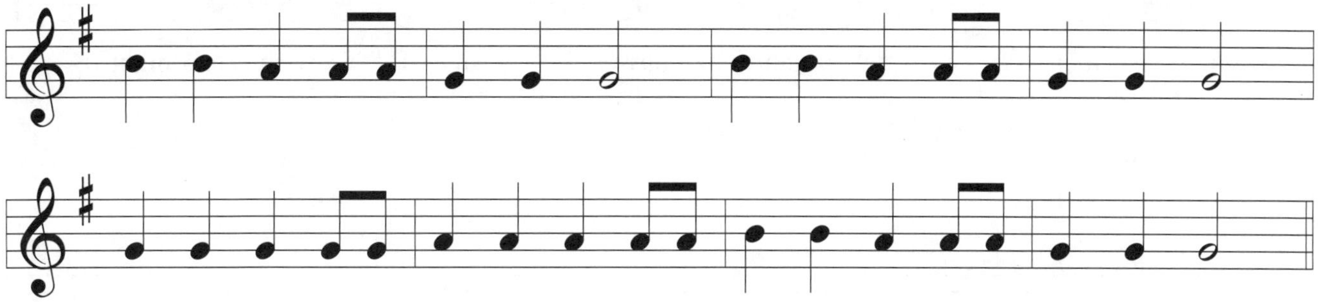

Variation 2:

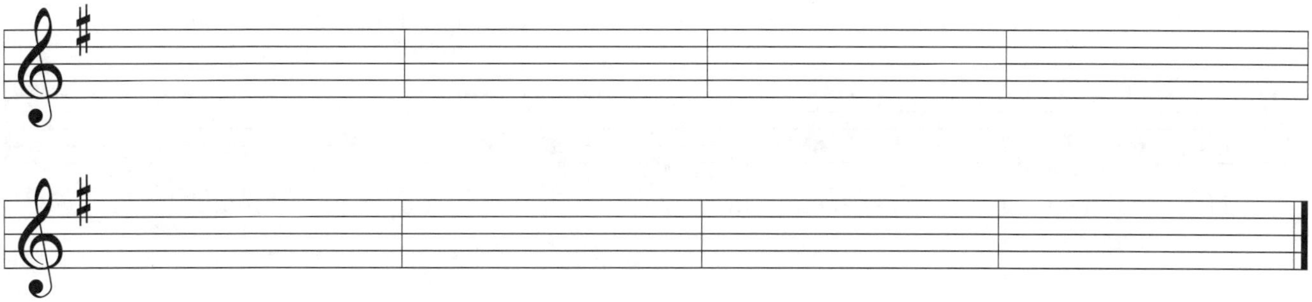

Wolfgang Amadeus Mozart

1756-1791

Mozart is often thought of as the most brilliant composer ever known. He was born in Austria in 1756. His father was one of the town's best music teachers, Leopold Mozart. By age four, Mozart began to study the keyboard and learned at an incredible rate. When Wolfgang was six, Leopold took his son and daughter on tour through the courts of Europe. When Wolfgang was seven, his first published works appeared. By age 13, Mozart had written *La Finta Semplis*, his first opera. In his 31 year musical career, Mozart wrote more than 600 works. Listen to some of Mozart's variations on "Ah vous dirais-je, Maman" K 265 on YouTube.

9. Starlight

2 bar intro

Traditional

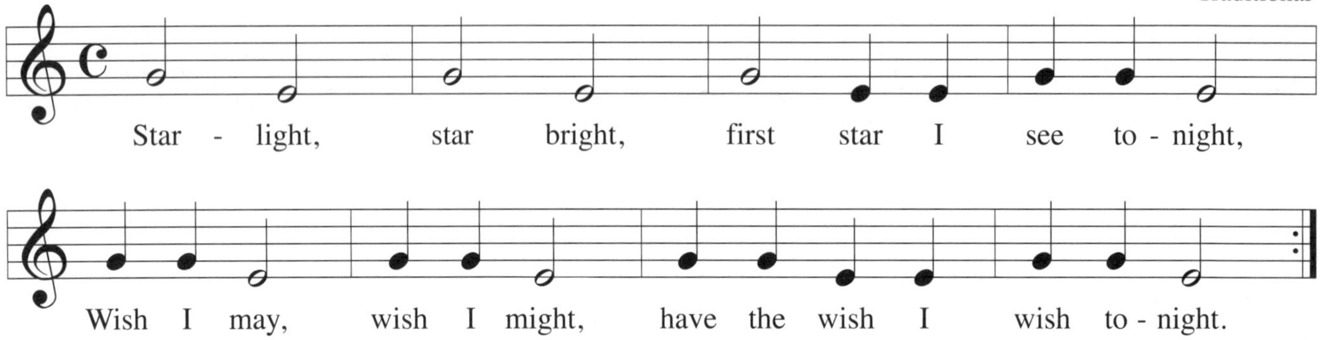

10. Lucy Locket

2 bar intro

Traditional

11. Kagome

2 bar intro

Japanese

12. BAGE Blues

2 bar intro

Denise Gagné

13. Little Tommy Tiddlemouse

2 bar intro

Traditional

Pickup Note: A pickup note is a note that comes before the first complete measure of music. In "Trampin'," count one, two, three and then play the B. The B is on beat four.

14. Trampin'

2 bar intro

Spiritual

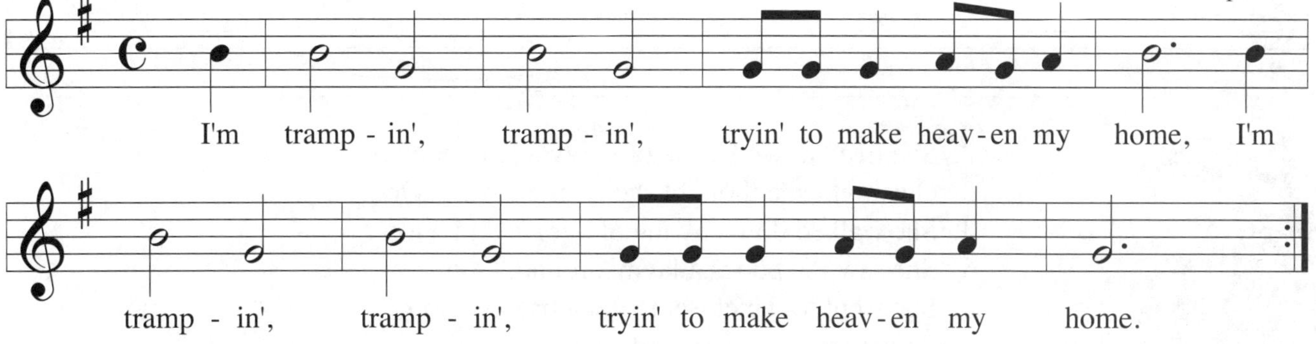

Slur: The curved line that connects different notes is a slur. This means to play without tonguing. Tongue the first note, then move your fingers to the next note(s) without tonguing.

15. Doggie Doggie

2 bar intro

16. Salish Hand Game

2 bar intro

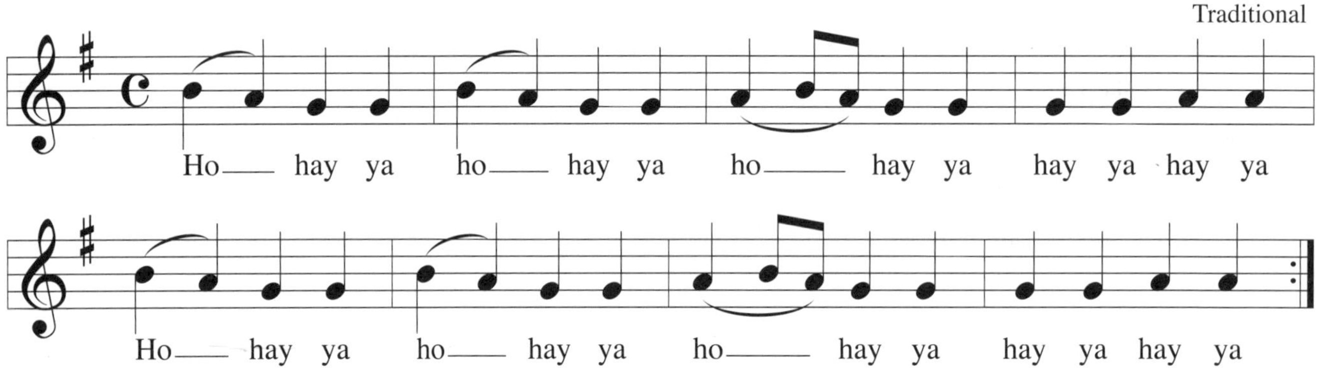

17. Skin and Bones

2 bar intro

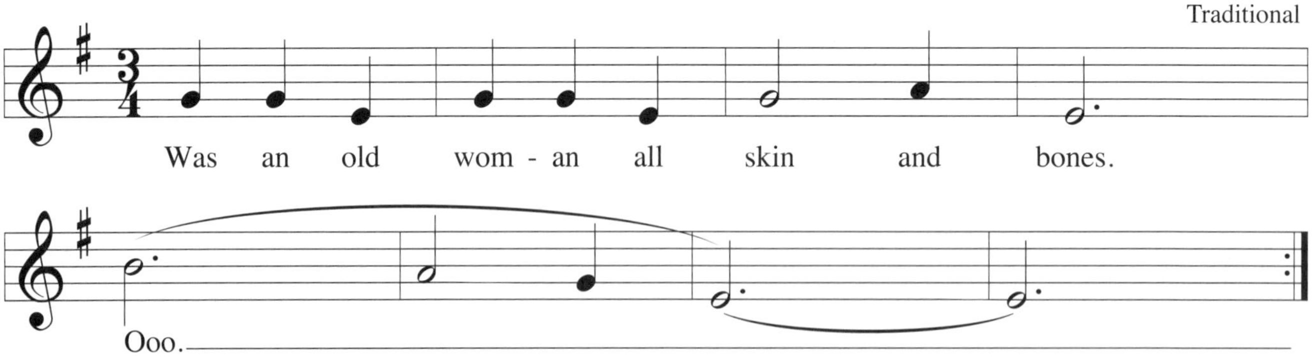

2. She lived down by the old graveyard. Ooo.
3. One night she thought she'd take a walk. Ooo.
4. She walked down by the old graveyard. Ooo.
5. She saw the bones a layin' around. Ooo.
6. She went to the closet to get a broom. Ooo.
7. She opened the door and BOO!

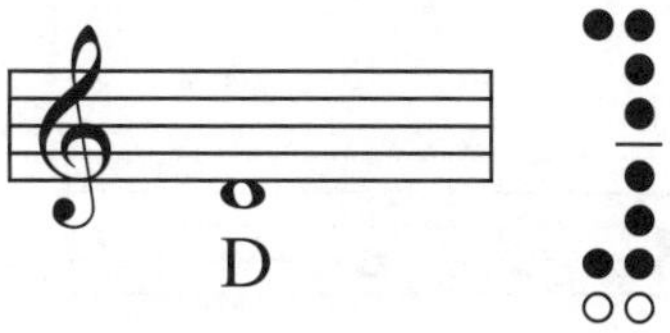

18. Frog in the Middle

2 bar intro

Traditional

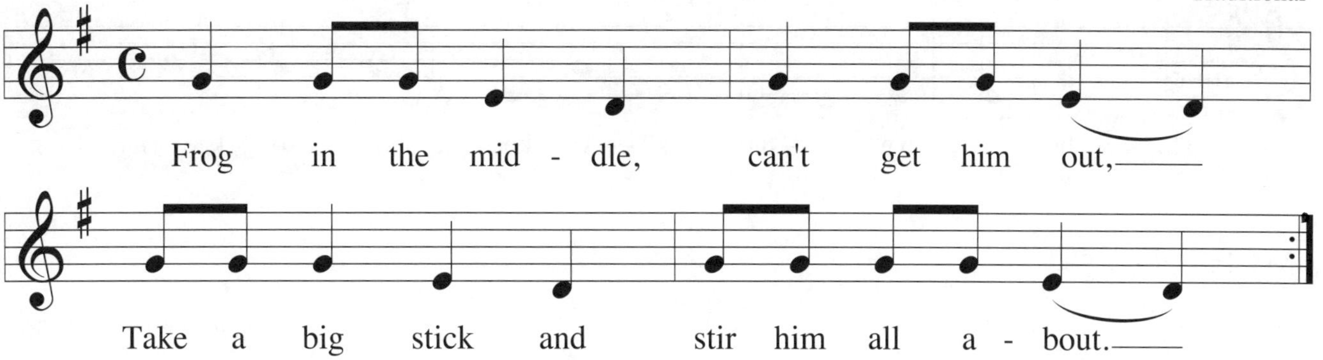

19. Country Swing

2 bar intro

Denise Gagné

Name Your Notes:

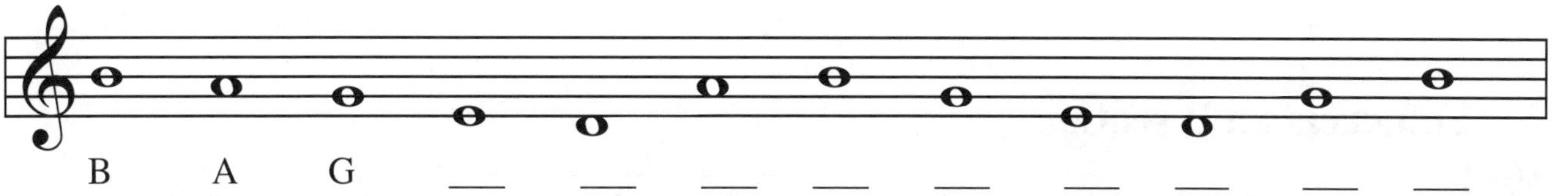

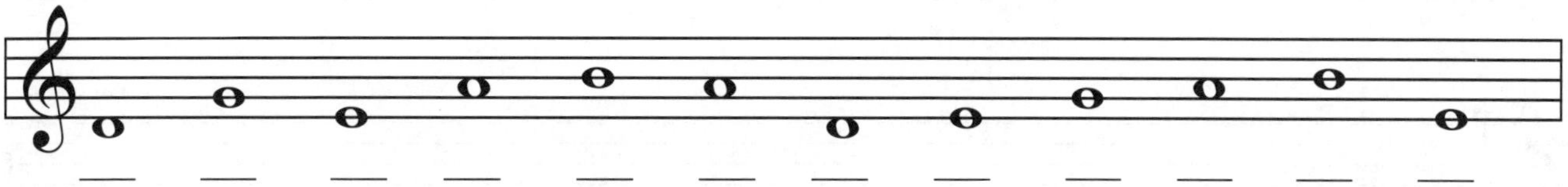

20. Ho Ho Watanay

2 bar intro

Iroquois

21. My Paddle

1 bar intro

Margaret Embers McGee

22. Rondo

2 bar intro

Denise Gagné

You create a B section

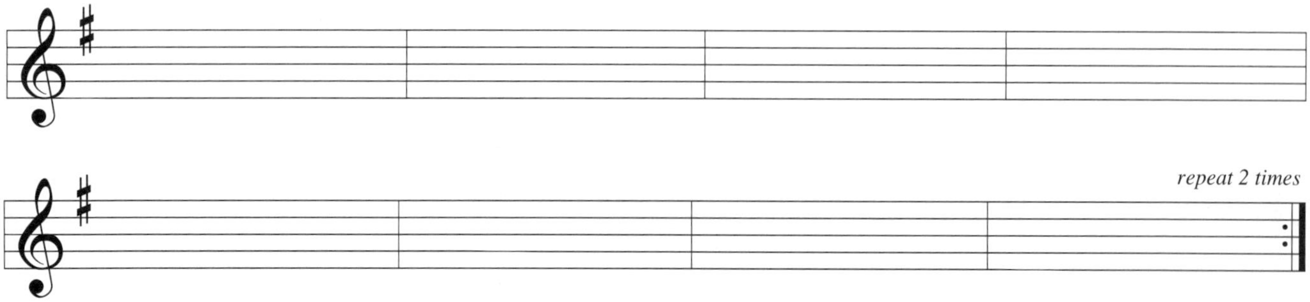

23. “C” You in Dixie

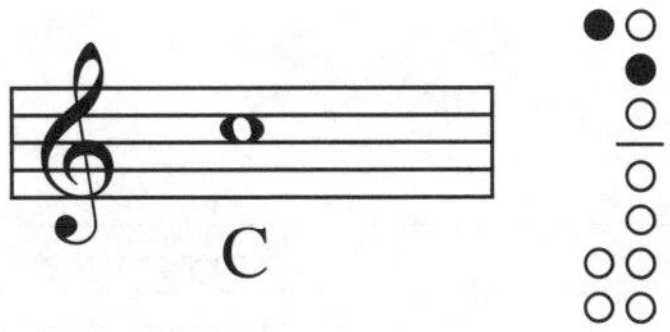

1 bar intro

Denise Gagné

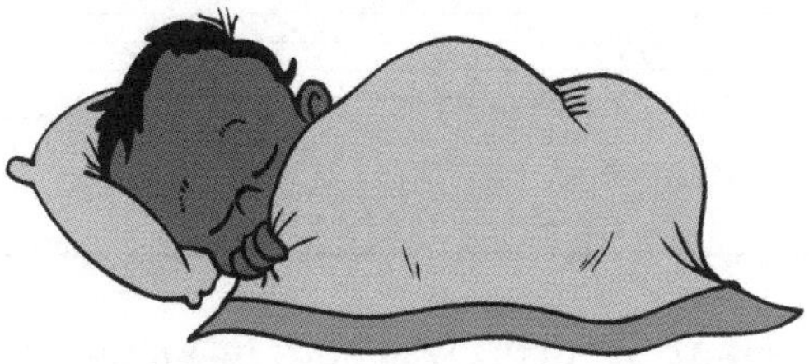

24. Hush Little Baby

2 bar intro

Traditional

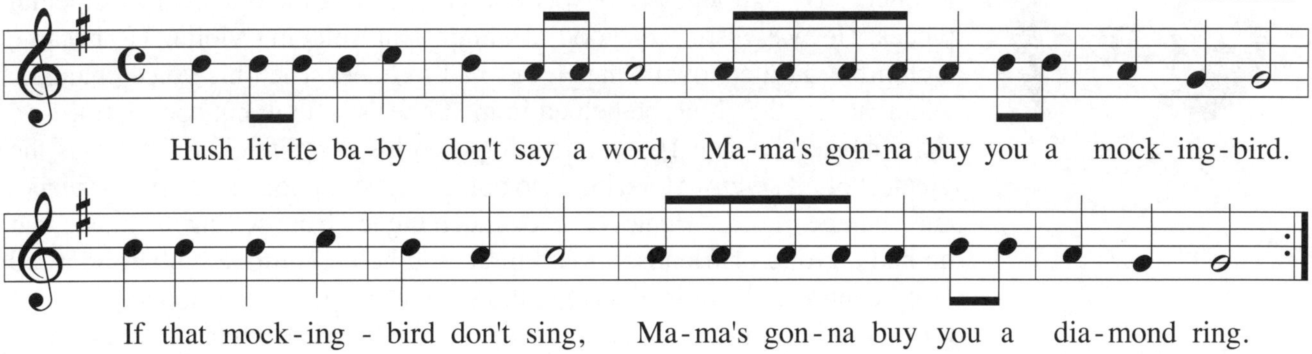

Name Your Notes:

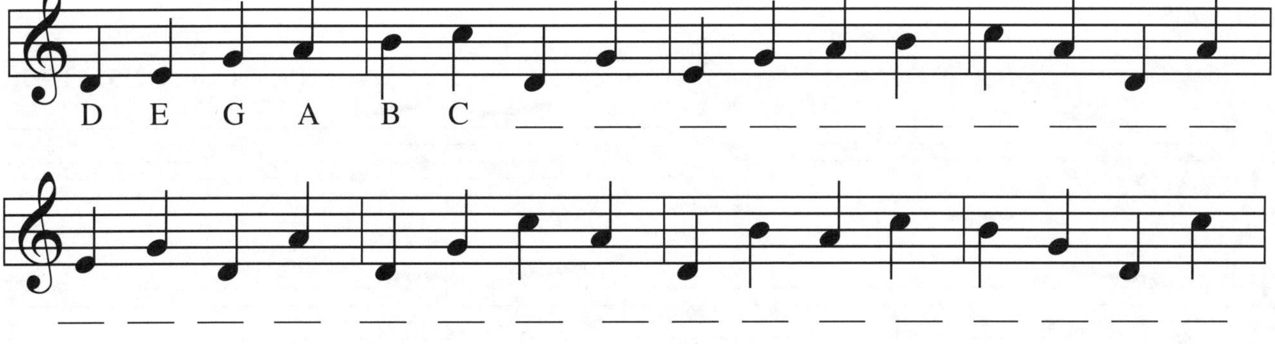

25. Sanctus

2 bar intro

Franz Schubert

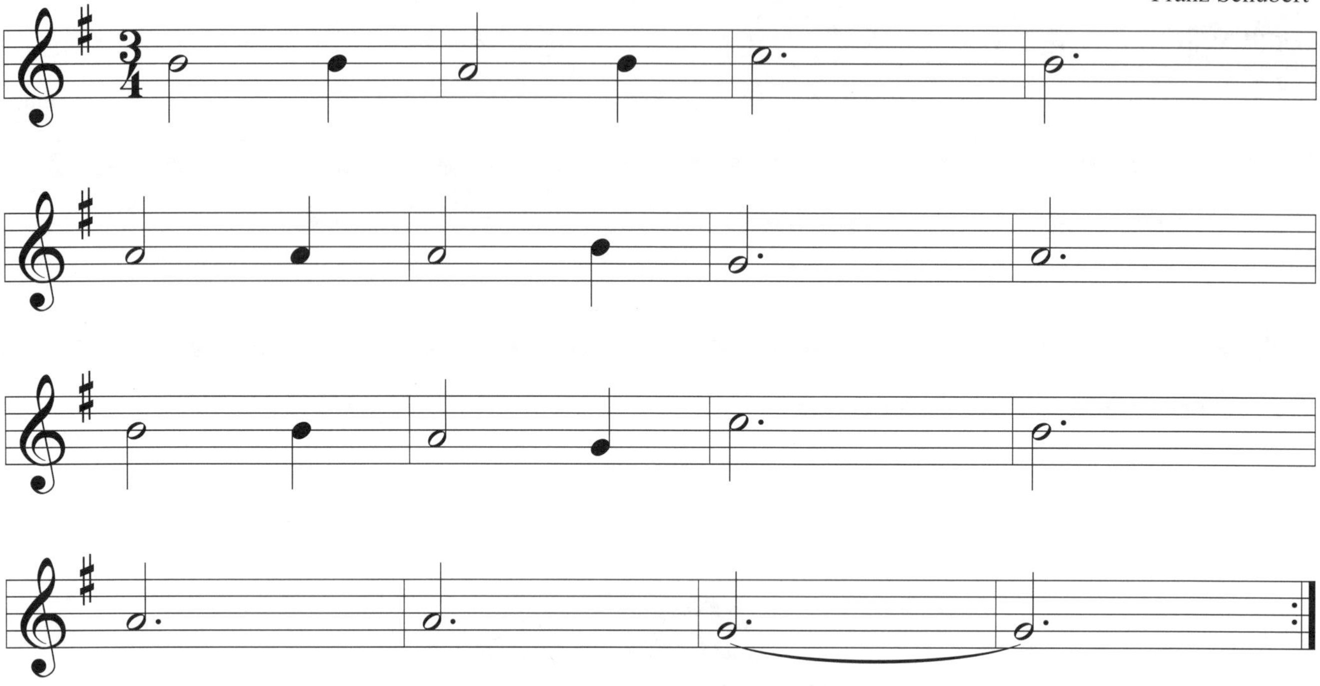

Franz Schubert
1797-1828

Franz Schubert was born in Vienna in 1797. His father was a schoolmaster whose large family loved and practiced music. His father was his first teacher. By age ten, Franz was composing songs and short instrumental pieces. He was also very good at singing and playing violin. He became a choirboy at the Royal Chapel, but had to leave when his voice changed. When he left the choir, he helped in his father's school, but soon left this to write music. By age 16, he had composed his first symphony! He was the greatest of all song writers, but also composed symphonies, music for piano, and chamber music. He never made much money from selling his music, but he had a group of friends who admired and helped him. Schubert admired Beethoven who lived in Vienna at the same time, but he was too shy to meet him. Schubert died when he was only 31. *Sanctus* is from the German Mass in F. Search for a performance of this movement on YouTube.

26. Bouffons

2 bar intro

Thoinot Arbeau (1519-1595)

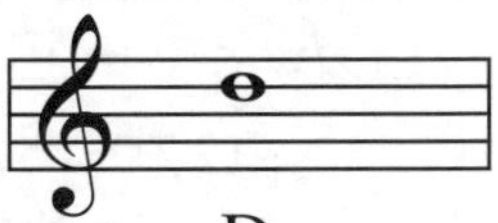

D

27. C and D

2 bar intro

Denise Gagné

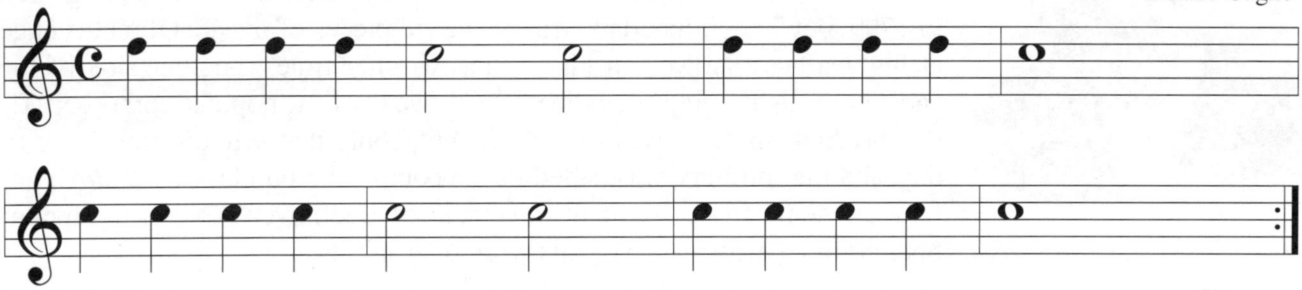

Johann Sebastian Bach

1685-1750

Johann Sebastian Bach was one of the greatest composers of the Baroque era. He was born in Germany more than 300 years ago. All of his family were good musicians. When he was in school, he was a choirboy. Later, he worked playing violin in a court orchestra, and organ in several different churches. Bach was the music director at the court of Prince Leopold. At the court, he wrote church music, music for instruments and books to teach his wife and children the keyboard. Bach's music is hard to play. The player must be able to play many fast notes. Some of his pieces are very slow and expressive. Bach wrote many cantatas for church services. "Jesu, Joy of Man's Desiring" is from Cantata 147 for chorus and orchestra. Search for a performance of this work on YouTube.

28. Jesu, Joy of Man's Desiring

4 bar intro

J.S. Bach

This is a whole rest. ▬ It is a whole measure of rest in any time signature. In "Jesu, Joy" there are three beats in each measure, so you will rest for three beats.

Ludwig van Beethoven

1770-1827

Ludwig van Beethoven was born in 1770. He grew up surrounded by music, as both his father and grandfather were local musicians. He became successful both as a pianist and as a composer. Beethoven began to go deaf in 1799, but he continued to write powerful pieces of music. Often his anger at his deafness showed in his music. At other times, another side of him showed in his flowing melodies. Beethoven was a popular composer. The day he died in 1827 was so sad for the people that schools closed for the day, and the military was called out to control the public. *Ode to Joy* is the famous theme from the final movement of Beethoven's Ninth Symphony. Search for a performance of this work on YouTube.

29. Ode to Joy

2 bar intro

Ludwig van Beethoven

30. Renaissance Round

2 bar intro

Renaissance

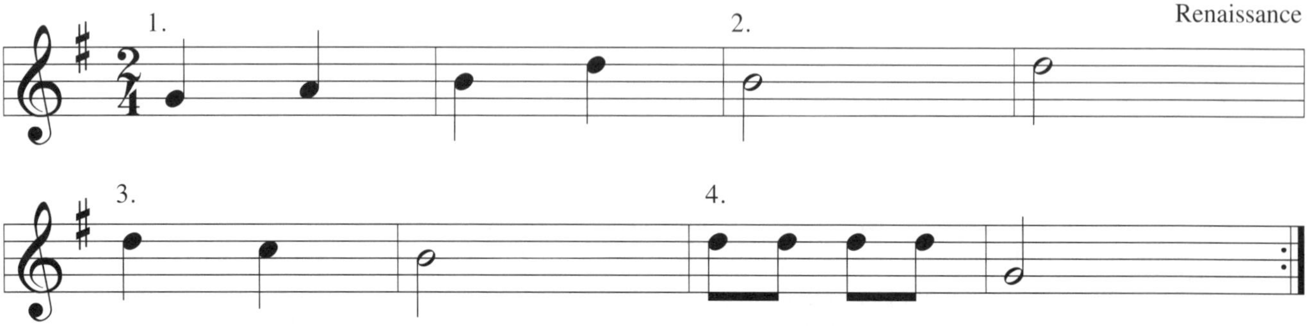

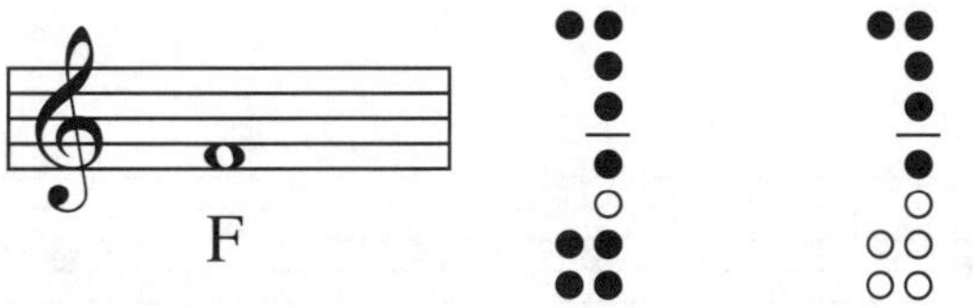

31. Closet Key

2 bar intro

Traditional

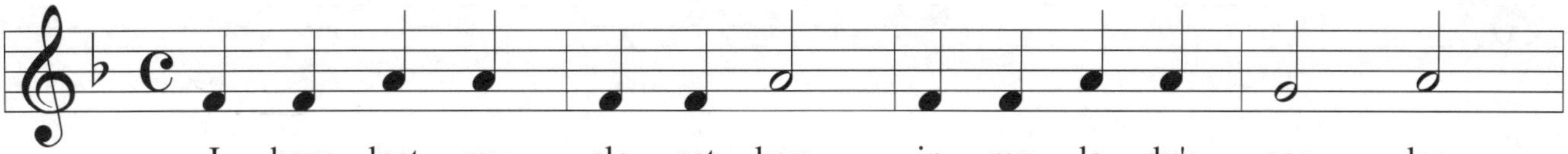

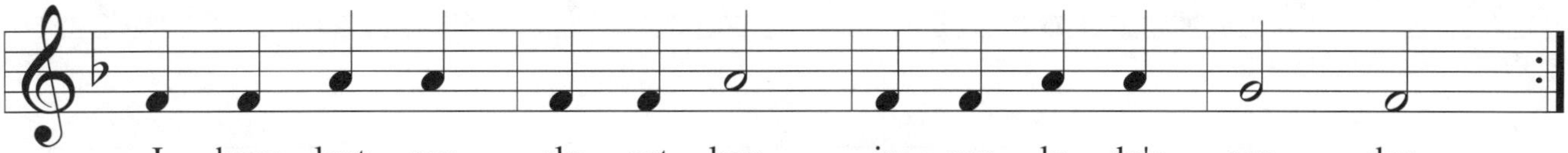

Antonin Dvorak

1841-1904

Dvorak was born in a village in Czechoslovakia. His father played the violin and sang, and Antonin studied music with the village school teacher. When he was 16, he went to Prague to study organ. When he finished school, he worked in Prague playing violin in a small orchestra and in the pit orchestra of the National Theater. He continued to study music and began composing, but his works weren't performed and he didn't make any money from them. Another great Czech composer, Smetana, began performing Dvorak's pieces. This helped Dvorak in his career. Another famous composer, Johannes Brahms, heard his music and also helped him in his career. Dvorak became famous throughout Europe and was often asked to conduct his works in other countries. He was hired to be the director of the National Conservatory in New York City, and lived in the United States for several years. His Symphony No. 9, *From the New World*, was written to celebrate the centennial of Columbus' discovery of America. Search for a performance of this work on YouTube.

32. From the New World

2 bar intro

Antonin Dvorak

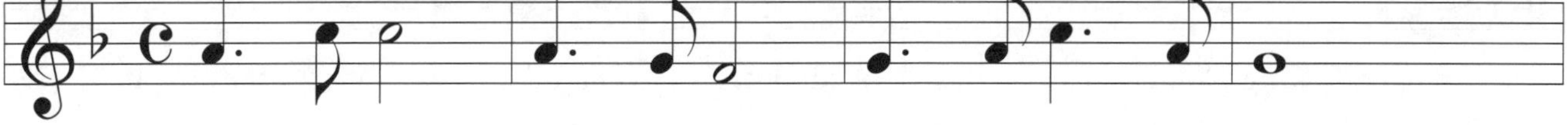

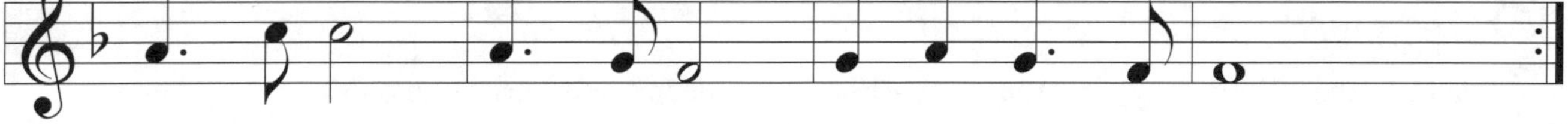

33. Morning

2 bar intro

Edvard Grieg

Edvard Grieg
1843-1907

Grieg was born in Norway in 1843. His mother was his first music teacher. Then he studied at the Leipzig Conservatory where he learned piano and musical theory. His music was romantic. He was a master of miniature musical forms. His music used the melodies and rhythms of Norway. This is called nationalism. Grieg worked to promote the music of Norway. In 1867 Grieg started the Norwegian Academy of Music. Because of his nationalistic style, the Norwegian government granted him an annual salary of 1600 crowns to help him write Norwegian music. His popularity throughout Europe increased and he was admired by such greats as Brahms and Tchaikovsky. Grieg was successful, but he was shy. He spent his later years away from public attention, though he continued to compose music. "Morning" is the theme of one of the movements of the *Peer Gynt Suite*. Grieg wrote this as incidental music for the play *Peer Gynt* by famous Norwegian author, Ibsen. Search for a performance of this work on YouTube.

34. Good King Wenceslas

2 bar intro

Traditional

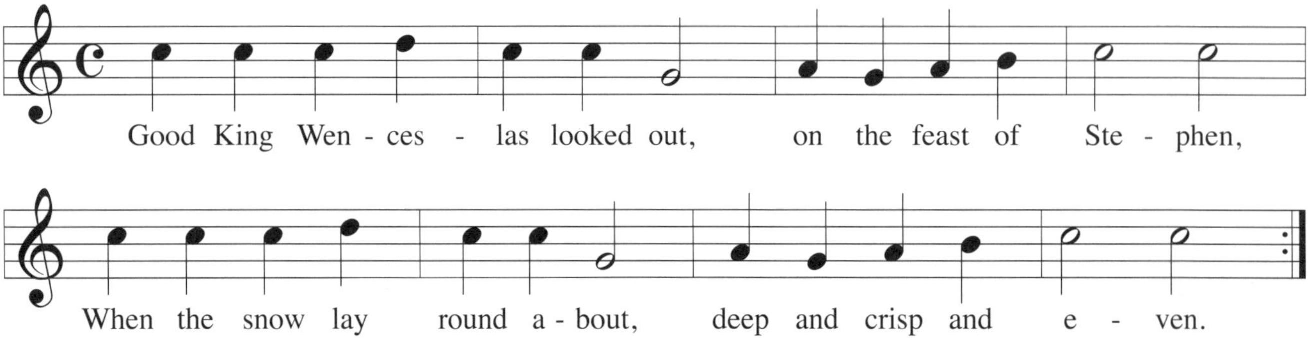

35. Jingle Bells

2 bar intro

James Pierpont

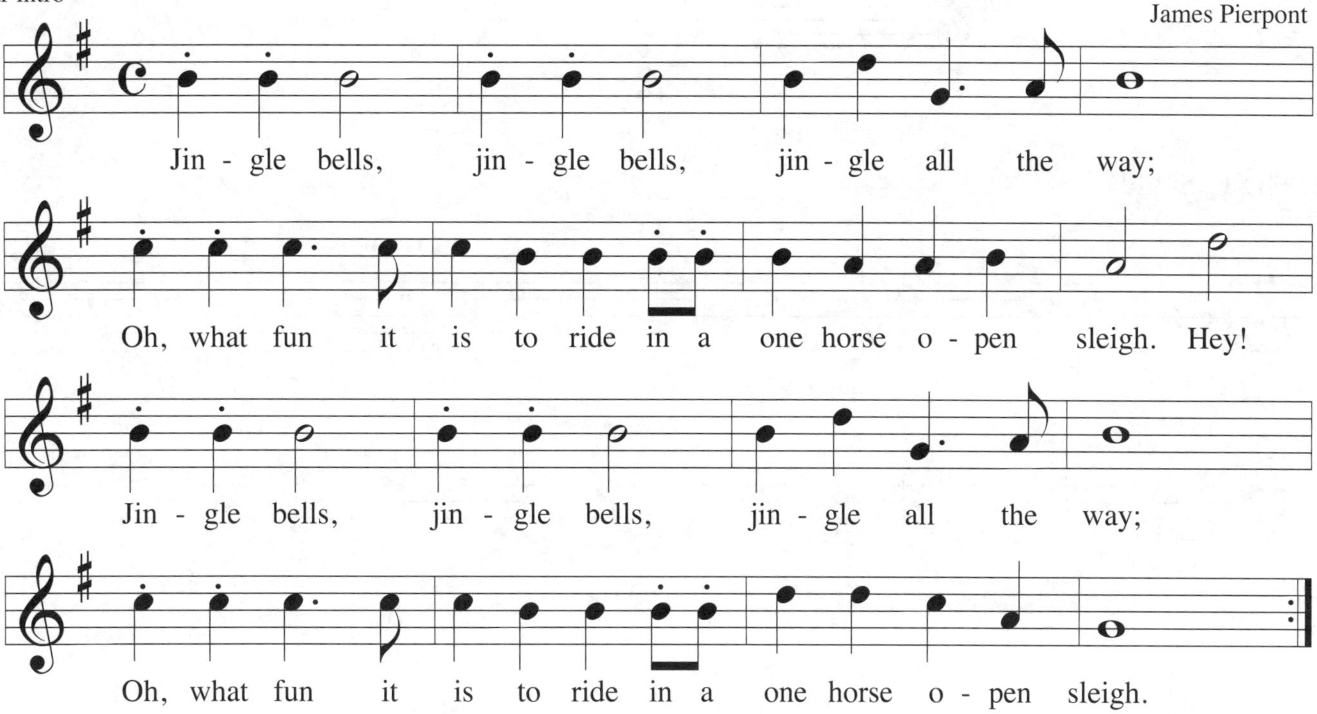

Staccato: A dot over or under a note indicates that the note is to be played staccato - in a detached style. Lightly tongue the note, separating it from the next note.

36. Jolly Old St. Nicholas

2 bar intro

Traditional

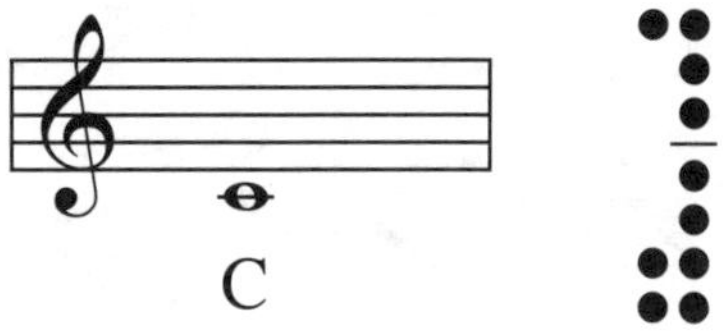

37. The C Scale

2 bar intro (repeats)

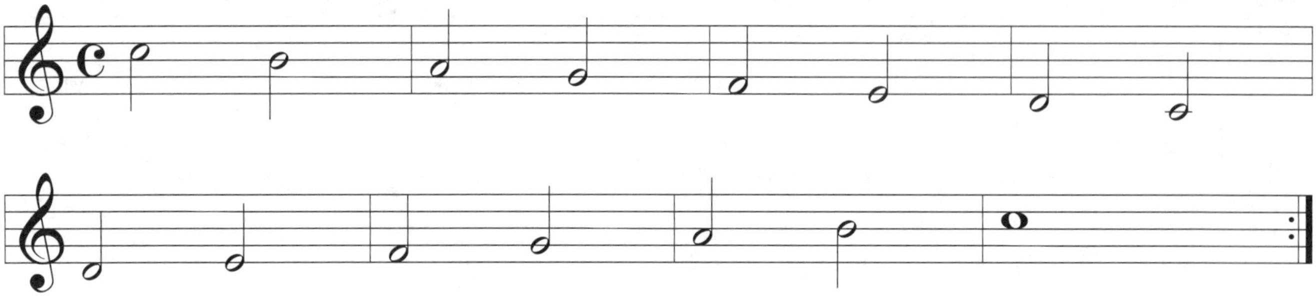

38. Camptown Races

2 bar intro (repeats)

Stephen Foster